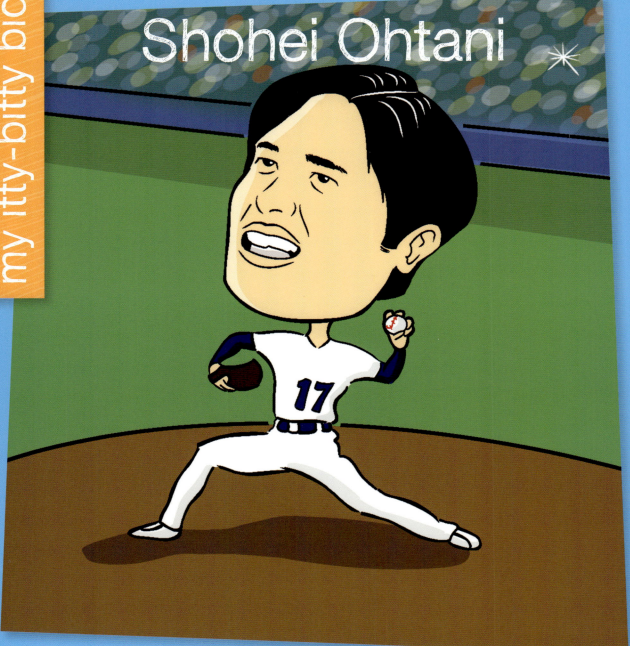

Published in the United States of America by Cherry Lake Publishing
Ann Arbor, Michigan
www.cherrylakepublishing.com

Reading Adviser: Beth Walker Gambro, MS, Ed., Reading Consultant, Yorkville, IL
Illustrator: Leo Trinidad

Photo Credits: © yspbqh14/Shutterstock, 5; © Angie Sidles/Shutterstock, 7; © The Yomiuri Shimbun via AP Images/ASSOCIATED PRESS, 9; © Image of sport/Alamy Stock Photo, 11; © UPI/Alamy Stock Photo, 13; © Aflo Co. Ltd./Alamy Stock Photo, 15, 22; © Aflo Co. Ltd./Alamy Stock Photo, 17; © Image of sport/Alamy Stock Photo, 19, 23; © Cal Sport Media/Alamy Stock Photo, 21

Copyright © 2026 by Cherry Lake Publishing
All rights reserved. No part of this book may be reproduced or utilized in
any form or by any means without written permission from the publisher.

Cherry Lake Press is an imprint of Cherry Lake Publishing Group

Library of Congress Cataloging-in-Publication Data has been filed and is available at catalog.loc.gov.

Printed in the United States of America

table of contents

My Story 4

Timeline 22

Glossary 24

Index 24

About the author: When not writing, Dr. Virginia Loh-Hagan serves as the Executive Director for AANAPISI Affairs and the APIDA Center at San Diego State University. She is also the Co-Executive Director of The Asian American Education Project. She lives in San Diego with her very tall husband and very naughty dogs.

About the illustrator: Leo Trinidad is a *New York Times* bestselling comic book artist, illustrator, and animator from Costa Rica. For more than 12 years, he's been creating content for children's books and TV shows. Leo created the first animated series ever produced in Central America and founded Rocket Cartoons, one of the most successful animation studios in Latin America. He is also the 2018 winner of the Central American Graphic Novel contest.

my story

I was born in 1994.
I am Japanese.

My last name means
"large valley."

Have you been to Japan

My family plays sports. We love baseball. I played at a young age.

My dad coached me.

I played in high school. I threw hard pitches.

I reached top speeds.

I play **professional** baseball. I played in Japan. I trained as a **two-way** player.

I can pitch. I can hit.

I moved to Los Angeles.

I played for the Angels and the Dodgers.

I won many games. I broke records. I won awards.

I am exciting to watch.

Do you watch sports?

I have fans in Japan. I have fans in the United States.

Still, I stay **humble**.

I hit 50 **home runs**. I stole 50 **bases**. I did this in one season.

I am the first to do this.

My legacy lives on. I am an **all-star** champ.

I shake things up.

What would you like to ask me?

timeline

2018

1980

Born
1994

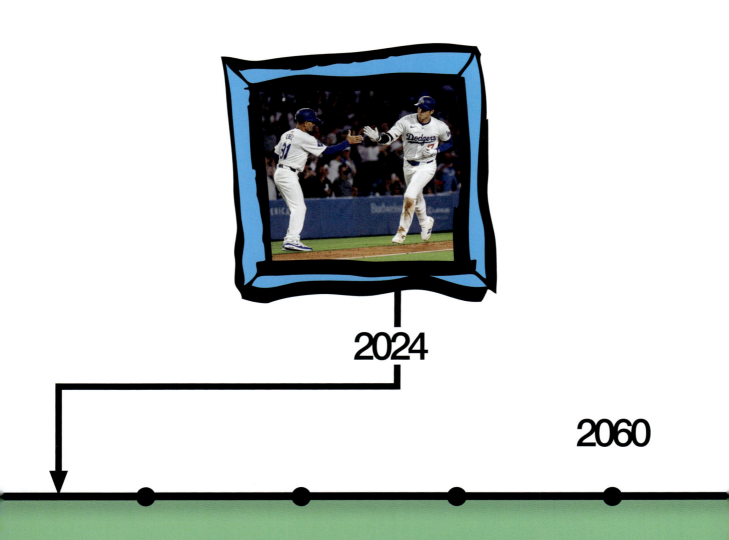

2024

2060

glossary

all-star (AWL-stahr) game between teams of top players chosen from different teams

bases (BAY-suhs) the four places on the infield that a player must touch in order to score a run

home runs (HOHM RUHNZ) baseball hits that allow the batter to circle the bases and reach home base in one play

humble (HUHM-buhl) respectful and not too proud

professional (pruh-FESH-nuhl) related to a job; describing when someone is paid for their work

two-way (TOO-WAY) able to play both offense and defense positions

index

baseball, 6–21
birth, 4, 22

family, 6
fans, 16–17

hitting, 10–11, 18

Japan, 4–5, 10, 16

Los Angeles Angels (team), 12–13, 15, 17
Los Angeles Dodgers (team), 11–12, 18–19, 21

pitching, 8–10, 13
professional career, 10–21

sports records, 18

talent, 8, 10–11, 14, 18, 20
timeline, 22–23